Koalas

by Joelle Riley

EARLY BIRD
NATURE BOOKS

Lerner Publications Company • Minneapolis

Lerner Publications Company
A division of Lerner Publishing Group
241 First Avenue North
Minneapolis, MN 55401   U.S.A.

Website address: www.lernerbooks.com

Library of Congress Cataloging-in-Publication Data

Riley, Joelle.
    Koalas / by Joelle Riley.
        p.   cm. — (Early bird nature books)
    Includes index.
    ISBN-13: 978–0–8225–2870–8 (lib. bdg. : alk. paper)
    ISBN-10: 0–8225–2870–3 (lib. bdg. : alk. paper)
    1. Koala—Juvenile literature. I. Title. II. Series.
QL737.M384R55 2006
599.2'5—dc22   2004028804

Manufactured in the United States of America
1 2 3 4 5 6 – JR – 11 10 09 08 07 06

Contents

Koalas live only in Australia. The red areas show exactly where koalas live.

Be a Word Detective

Can you find these words as you read about the koala's life? Be a detective and try to figure out what they mean. You can turn to the glossary on page 46 for help.

arboreal

extinct

home range

joeys

marsupials

nocturnal

pap

poisonous

pouch

vitamins

Chapter 1

Koalas usually stay up in the treetops. What are the koala's closest relatives?

The Cuddly Koala

A koala sits high up in a tree. It looks like a cuddly teddy bear. The koala's body is round and furry. Large, fuzzy ears stick out from its head. The koala has round, brown eyes. Its nose is big and black.

Some people call this animal a "koala bear." But the koala is not a bear. The koala's closest relatives are wombats, possums, and opossums. Koalas, wombats, and possums all live in Australia. Opossums live in North America and South America.

Opossums are close relatives of koalas.

Koalas and their relatives are marsupials (mar-SOO-pee-uhls). This group of animals all produce their young the same way. Baby marsupials grow inside their mother's body for a very short time. They are tiny when they are born. They grow bigger inside a pouch on their mother's body.

Kangaroos are marsupials. You can see the baby kangaroo peeking its head out of its mother's pouch.

Koalas have round bodies. But they are not fat.

An adult koala looks soft and round. But its body is strong. A full-grown male koala is about 2 feet long. It weighs 20 to 30 pounds. Female koalas are a little smaller than males.

A koala's thick fur keeps it warm in cold, wet weather.

Soft, thick fur covers the koala's body. Most of the fur is gray or grayish brown. White fur grows on its throat, on its belly, and inside its ears. Fur keeps the koala warm in cold weather and dry in wet weather. Rain can't soak through the thick fur.

10

Koalas have long, strong legs. They use their legs and feet to climb trees. Each of the koala's feet has five toes. Rough pads cover the bottoms of the feet.

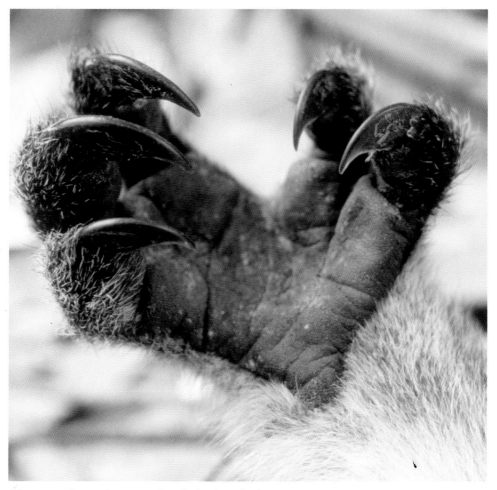

The rough pads on a koala's feet help it climb trees.

The koala's front feet are different from its back feet. Each front foot has two toes on one side and three toes on the other side. The foot looks sort of like a person's hand would look if it had two thumbs and three fingers. The koala holds onto things with its toes the way people grip things in their hands. All the toes on the koala's front feet have long, sharp claws.

You can see the two "thumbs" on this koala's front foot.

The koala's feet are made for climbing trees.

A koala's feet have long claws.

Each back foot has a short, stubby big toe. This toe does not have a claw. The other four toes are longer and have claws. Two of the long toes on each back foot are joined together, except for the tips. Koalas use the tips like a comb. They comb their fur to keep it soft and clean.

The koala has thick fur on its rump. The fur is like a pillow. This padding helps koalas sit on hard tree branches while they sleep, rest, and eat.

A koala leans back and relaxes as it munches on some leaves.

Chapter 2

Koalas live in trees. How does a koala move from tree to tree?

Living in the Trees

Koalas are arboreal (ar-BOR-ee-uhl). Arboreal animals spend most of their time in trees. Koalas live in eucalyptus (yoo-kuh-LIHP-tuhs) trees. Koalas use their strong claws to hold onto branches and tree trunks. They jump from one tree to the next.

Sometimes a tree is too far away. Then a koala won't jump. It climbs down to the ground instead. The koala walks to the next tree. It sways back and forth as it walks. Then it quickly scoots up the trunk of the tree.

Koalas are better at climbing than they are at walking on the ground.

A koala perches on a branch.

Koalas eat mainly eucalyptus leaves. These thick leaves are poisonous to most animals. But koalas can eat them without getting sick. Koalas eat about 1 pound of eucalyptus leaves every day. That's about as much as one head of lettuce.

Koalas eat leaves that are poisonous to other animals.

Koalas are picky eaters. They sniff eucalyptus leaves carefully before they eat. Koalas have a very good sense of smell. They can tell which leaves are the best to eat. Koalas will eat only the newest and tastiest leaves. They nip off the leaves with their sharp front teeth. Then they grind the leaves with their back teeth.

The koala's back teeth are good for grinding leaves.

Koalas get most of the water they need from the eucalyptus leaves they eat.

Eucalyptus leaves have a lot of water inside them. And at night, dew forms on the leaves. Dew is drops of water from the air. Koalas hardly ever drink water. In fact, the name *koala* means "no drink." Koalas get the water they need when they eat leaves.

Koalas spend most of the day sleeping.

Eucalyptus leaves do not have many vitamins. So koalas don't get much energy from their food. They usually move slowly, and they sleep a lot. Koalas sleep up to 18 hours a day. They sleep on branches high in the trees.

Koalas are nocturnal (nok-TUR-nuhl).
Nocturnal animals are active at night. Koalas
sleep during the day. They look for food at night.

*Koalas are active
after the sun goes
down.*

Chapter 3

Koalas usually live alone. How does a koala tell other koalas where it lives?

Koalas at Home

Koalas live in forests on the east coast of Australia. Adult koalas usually live alone. Each koala chooses its own part of a forest to live in. This area is the koala's home range. A home range has enough trees to supply the food and shelter a koala needs.

A koala marks its home range. It wants other koalas to know where it lives. The koala goes from tree to tree around the edges of its home range. It uses its claws to make scratches on the trees. Other koalas see the scratches. They know the trees belong to another koala.

Koalas live in forests in Australia.

Male koalas also rub against trees to mark their home ranges. An adult male koala has a brown spot in the middle of his white chest. The brown spot is smelly liquid. The male koala rubs his chest on a tree. The smelly liquid stays on the tree. Other koalas can smell the liquid. They know the tree is part of the male koala's home range.

Adult male koalas have a brown spot on their chests.

Young koalas live in their mother's home range.

Males usually share their home ranges with female koalas. But male koalas do not like other males to come into their home ranges. Koalas usually live alone in their home range their whole life. But they sometimes meet other koalas at the borders of their home range.

Chapter 4

Baby koalas are called joeys (JOH-eez). When are joeys born?

Baby Koalas

Female koalas usually have one baby each year. A baby koala is called a joey. Joeys are born in the spring or the summer.

A newborn joey is tiny. It looks sort of like a pink jelly bean. The joey has no hair or teeth. It can smell and touch, but it can't hear or see. The joey's front legs are strong, but its back legs are very weak.

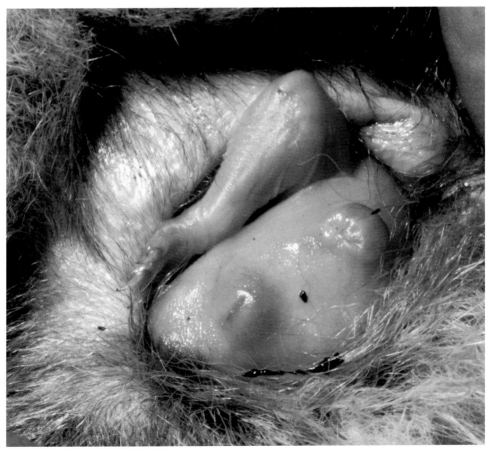

A newborn joey does not have any fur. Its eyes are not yet open, but it can smell and touch.

The newborn joey uses its front legs to hang onto its mother's fur. It crawls by grabbing and pulling on the fur. The joey smells where it should go. It crawls across its mother's stomach and into her pouch. The pouch keeps the joey safe and warm.

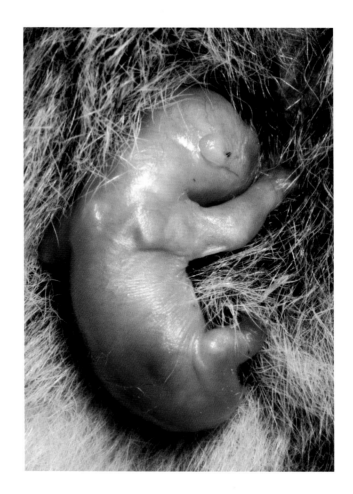

A joey holds on to its mother's fur to climb across her belly and into her pouch.

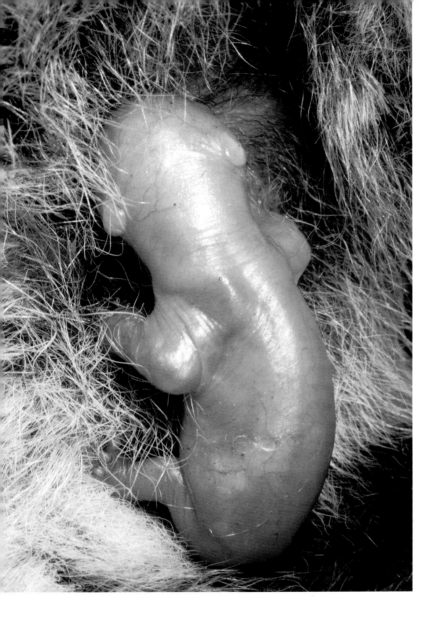

A young joey eats only its mother's milk.

Inside the mother koala's pouch are two teats. The teats make milk. The joey grabs a teat with its mouth and starts to drink. The joey stays on the teat for about four months.

This joey peeks its head out from its mother's pouch.
It has already grown fur all over its body.

The joey drinks milk and grows fast. Soon it has some fur. The joey's back legs grow stronger. But its eyes are still closed.

The joey opens its eyes when it is about five months old. It starts to peek out of its mother's pouch. But the joey stays in the pouch and drinks milk. The mother koala starts to give the joey a special food called pap. Pap is soft and mushy. It comes from eucalyptus leaves that the mother koala chewed and ate. Eating pap helps the joey grow faster.

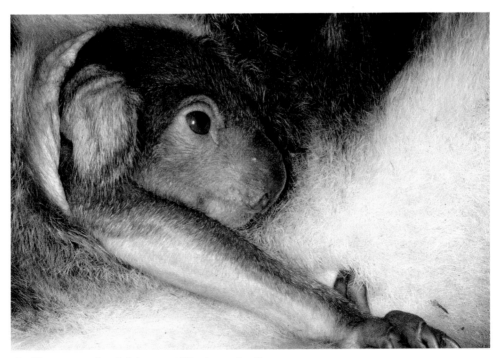

A five-month-old joey still stays in its mother's pouch.

When the joey is six months old, its fur is thick. Its teeth have started to grow. The joey climbs out of the pouch. It holds onto the fur on its mother's stomach. It rides with her wherever she goes. The joey often returns to the pouch to drink milk and to sleep.

Joeys stay close to their mothers.

Older joeys ride on their mothers' backs.

At seven months old, the joey is nearly too big to fit in its mother's pouch. It starts to ride on her back. As its mother eats, the joey nibbles on leaves. It watches its mother choose which leaves to eat. The joey learns how to find the tastiest leaves.

This nine-month-old joey is ready to start exploring on its own.

When the joey is nine months old, it begins to climb around by itself. It explores the trees. But it always stays close to its mother. It eats eucalyptus leaves. But sometimes it drinks milk too.

When the young koala is one year old, it is ready to live on its own. It lives in its mother's home range until it is about two years old. Then it leaves. The young koala looks for a home range of its own.

Koalas start living on their own when they are one year old.

Chapter 5

*People have caused
the main dangers
that koalas face.
How have people
hurt koalas?*

Koalas in Danger

 The koala's main enemy is people.
People hunted and killed millions of koalas long
ago. They used the koala's thick fur for clothing.

Fewer and fewer koalas were left. People
began to worry that koalas would become
extinct (ek-STINGT). When a kind of animal is
extinct, it is gone forever. People made laws to
protect koalas. The laws said that people could
no longer hunt koalas.

But koalas are still in danger. Once there were huge forests of eucalyptus trees in Australia. Over time, people have cut down most of the trees. They have built houses and roads where the forests used to be. Koalas don't have as many trees to live in.

Many koalas are hit by cars when they try to walk across roads. This sign tells drivers to watch out for koalas on the road.

Koalas have to find a new place to live when they run out of food.

The big forests had plenty of food for koalas. But smaller forests don't have as many eucalyptus trees. It is harder for koalas to find food. A koala has to leave its home range when it runs out of food. The koala walks around and looks for a new home range.

40

Koalas are safe in the treetops. But they are not safe on the ground. Many koalas get hit by cars when they try to cross roads. Some koalas are killed by people's pet dogs. Other koalas drown. They fall into swimming pools and can't climb out.

Koalas need trees for food and safety.

The people of Australia want to protect koalas. They have made parks where koalas are safe. They have also built hospitals where doctors help hurt or sick koalas.

Doctors help koalas that are hurt or sick.

People can help make sure that koalas have what they need to survive.

People around the world care about koalas too. They are working hard to help these lovable animals. They want koalas to always have safe places to live and plenty of eucalyptus leaves to eat.

On Sharing a Book

As you know, adults greatly influence a child's attitude toward reading. When a child sees you read, or when you share a book with a child, you're sending a message that reading is important. Show the child that reading a book together is important to you. Find a comfortable, quiet place. Turn off the television and limit other distractions, such as telephone calls.

Be prepared to start slowly. Take turns reading parts of this book. Stop and talk about what you're reading. Talk about the photographs. You may find that much of the shared time is spent discussing just a few pages. This discussion time is valuable for both of you, so don't move through the book too quickly. If the child begins to lose interest, stop reading. Continue sharing the book at another time. When you do pick up the book again, be sure to revisit the parts you have already read. Most importantly, enjoy the book!

Be a Vocabulary Detective

You will find a word list on page 5. Words selected for this list are important to the understanding of the topic of this book. Encourage the child to be a word detective and search for the words as you read the book together. Talk about what the words mean and how they are used in the sentence. Do any of these words have more than one meaning? You will find these words defined in a glossary on page 46.

What about Questions?

Use questions to make sure the child understands the information in this book. Here are some suggestions:

> What is this paragraph about? What does this picture show? What do you think we'll learn about next? Could a koala live in your backyard? Why or why not? Why does the koala move so slowly? Why is the koala good at living in trees? What do you think it's like to be a koala? Why are people the biggest threat to koalas? What is your favorite part of the book? Why?

If the child has questions, don't hesitate to respond with questions of your own, such as What do *you* think? Why? What is it that you don't know? If the child can't remember certain facts, turn to the index.

Introducing the Index

The index is an important learning tool. It helps readers get information quickly without searching throughout the whole book. Turn to the index on page 47. Choose an entry, such as *feet*, and ask the child to use the index to find out how the koala uses its feet. Repeat this exercise with as many entries as you like. Ask the child to point out the differences between an index and a glossary. (The index helps readers find information quickly, while the glossary tells readers what words mean.)

Where in the World?

Many plants and animals found in the Early Bird Nature Books series live in parts of the world other than the United States. Encourage the child to find the places mentioned in this book on a world map or globe. Take time to talk about climate, terrain, and how you might live in such places.

All the World in Metric!

Although our monetary system is in metric units (based on multiples of 10), the United States is one of the few countries in the world that does not use the metric system of measurement. Here are some conversion activities you and the child can do using a calculator:

WHEN YOU KNOW:	MULTIPLY BY:	TO FIND:
miles	1.609	kilometers
feet	0.3048	meters
inches	2.54	centimeters
gallons	3.785	liters
tons	0.907	metric tons
pounds	0.454	kilograms

Activities

Visit a zoo to see different kinds of marsupials, such as koalas, kangaroos, wombats, possums, and opossums. How are these animals similar? How are they different?

Make up a story about a koala. Use the information in this book. Draw or paint pictures to illustrate your story.

Koalas don't move much. They sit on hard tree branches for hours at a time. See how long you can sit still on a hard floor or a hard chair.

Glossary

arboreal (ar-BOR-ee-uhl): living in trees

extinct (ek-STINGT): gone forever. When a type of animal dies out, it is extinct.

home range: the area in which a koala lives

joeys (JOH-eez): baby koalas

marsupials (mar-SOO-pee-uhls): members of a group of animals that include koalas and kangaroos. All female marsupials carry their young in a pouch.

nocturnal (nok-TUR-nuhl): active at night

pap: soft food for baby koalas made up of eucalyptus leaves the mother koala ate

poisonous: having a substance that can cause sickness or death

pouch: a flap of skin on a marsupial's stomach. Baby marsupials grow in the pouch after they are born.

vitamins: substances in food needed for good health

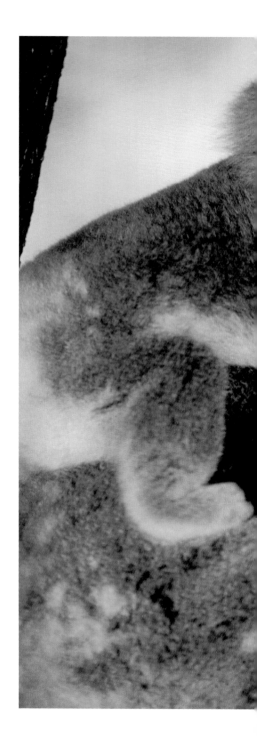

Index

Pages listed in **bold** type refer to photographs.

About the Author

Joelle Riley is an author and editor of children's books. She lives in Minneapolis, Minnesota, with her two greyhounds and two cats. Her books for Lerner Publications Company include *Buzzing Bumblebees, Pouncing Bobcats, Quiet Owls,* and *The Nervous System.*

gift 11/15   2 1/16   3 3/21